FROM GRIEF TO GRATEFULNESS

A Journey of Hope

Richard Exley

VALLEW
PRESS

13 12 11 10 09 08   10 9 8 7 6 5 4 3 2 1

From Grief to Gratefulness
—A Journey of Hope
ISBN 1-59379-118-6
Copyright © 2008 by Richard Exley
P.O. Box 54744
Tulsa, Oklahoma 74155

Published by **Vallew Press**
P.O. Box 35327
Tulsa, Oklahoma 74153-0327

In memory of
Ben Roy Wallace, Jr.,
Richard Orville Exley,
and Jack Ingram
men of God,
fathers,
and friends.

Contents

Introduction 7

Chapter 1   *The Shadow of Death* 15

Chapter 2   *The Journey Begins* 33

Chapter 3   *Temptations Along the Way* 51

Chapter 4   *The Power of His Presence* 73

Chapter 5   *From Grief to Gratefulness* 95

Epilogue 111

Appendix   *Prayers for Those Who Grieve* 119

            *A Prayer to Pray When
            the Prognosis is Grim* 119

            *A Prayer to Pray When You
            Can't Feel God's Presence* 120

            *A Prayer to Pray When Grief
            Tempts You to be Angry* 121

            A Prayer for Assurance 122

            A Prayer for Gratefulness 123

            A Prayer of Thanksgiving 124

Endnotes 125

About the Author 127

INTRODUCTION

My heart hurts as I write this and my eyes are damp with tears. In the past twenty-eight months, three of the most important men in my life have gone to be with the Lord. Brenda's father, Ben Roy Wallace, Jr., passed away on April 21, 2005. My father died on February 8, 2007, and on June 20th of this year my dear friend, Jack Ingram, went to be with the Lord.

Nearly all of this book was written before either my father or Jack Ingram passed away and therefore it does not address their deaths or the grief they occasioned, except in a most cursory way. You may be assured, however, that I am once again walking through the valley of the shadow of death, a journey not unlike the one I took following Ben Roy's death and I fully expect that in the end, my grief will once again be turned into gratefulness.

I won't lie to you. There have been times when the pain was nearly more than I could bear but always God sustained me. He did not take the pain away, but He gave me the strength to bear it. And as great as my grief has been God's grace has been greater still.

The Lord is no respecter of persons[1] and what He has done for me during the months of my grief, gives me confidence to know He will do the same for you. No matter how much you are suffering, I can assure you that God will see you through.

He is the "*…Father of compassion and the God of all comfort, who comforts us in all our troubles…*"[2]

But I must remind you that grief's healing work is a cooperative effort between you and the Lord. He is faithful but He can't turn your grief into gratefulness without your cooperation.

The first thing I had to do was ask for help and I want to encourage you to reach out to the Lord and to others in your time of sorrow. Remember, it is not weakness but wisdom that causes us to seek help rather than trying to go it alone. Even though no one can undo what death has done, a compassionate friend affords you at least two sources of encouragement—prayer and presence. In the time of grief a friend can sustain you as nothing else can. It's often the way God works—*"But God, who comforts the downcast, comforted us by the coming of Titus."*[3]

Early on, I realized that I would have to choose between the infallible Word of God and my volatile emotions. Had I trusted my emotions, I would have surely despaired for there were times when they were all over the place. At times, it felt like I was alone, as if God had abandoned me in the hour of my greatest need. At other times my overwrought emotions told me God could not be trusted, that God didn't care and that I would never get over my loss.

Had I not clung tenaciously to the truth of Scripture in those dark hours I would have surely lost my way. But by an act of my will I chose to trust God even when grief made it impossible for me to understand His ways and like an unerring compass His Word guided me through the fog of grief.

For weeks on end it seemed I had little or no energy. All I wanted to do was withdraw from life but I gritted my teeth and refused to stop living. And as I continued to force myself to do the things I knew to do, my zest for living began to return, not all at once but little by little.

Based on my personal experience I strongly encourage you to keep doing the things you know are right, no matter how artificial they may feel. Doubt if you must. Question if you will. But whatever

you do, don't give up. Go through the
motions if that is all you can do, for in
time your motions will have meaning. Not
all at once but over time, until one day
you discover that you are beginning to feel
alive again. At least that's the way it has
been for me.

Finally, I offered a sacrifice of praise.
It wasn't easy to worship in the time of
grief, but it was absolutely mandatory. It
was the only way I could put my sorrow
into perspective. No matter how bad the
situation, I discovered there is always
something for which we can be thankful,
something for which we can praise the
Lord. If you focus on that, rather than on
your loss, you will discover hope, even in
the midst of the most despairing grief.

The sacrifice of praise did not alter my painful circumstances one whit, but it did put them into eternal perspective. Seen through the lens of our grief, God appears small and far away—like looking at Him through the wrong end of a telescope. The sacrifice of praise turns the telescope around. It changes our focus. Now, God is near and a very present help in the time of trouble.[4]

These are the things I have learned, the truths that have sustained me during the dark hours of my grief. I offer them to you as a gift to strengthen you as you journey through the valley of the shadow of death. You are not alone. We are companions on this journey and I am praying for you. May the promise of His presence and the hope

of eternal life give you comfort as you
move *From Grief to Gratefulness.*

—Richard Exley

Chapter 1

THE SHADOW OF DEATH

I was fifty-eight years old and my wife just a year younger when the shadow of death fell across our immediate family, although it was not to become a reality until six months later. We became aware of its lurking presence in October, when the surgeon informed us that the tumor he had removed from Brenda's father's colon was malignant. Subsequent tests revealed that the cancer had already spread to his lymph glands. According to the doctor, Ben could expect to live no more than six to twelve months.

With all four of our parents nearing the age of eighty, we knew something like this was bound to happen sooner or later. Still, nothing had prepared us for the emotional impact we experienced when this hypothetical possibility became a harsh reality. After the initial shock wore off, we found ourselves vacillating between a fragile hope and a numbing despair. Maybe the Lord would heal Ben. Maybe the doctors were wrong. At other times we found ourselves lying awake at night, sick with dread, as we tried to imagine life without him.

Looking at Ben, four weeks after his surgery, it was hard to believe that he had only a few months to live. He appeared to be the picture of health. Although he was seventy-eight years old he still stood tall, his posture erect. His face was mostly unlined and he had a nearly full head of beautiful white hair. Already he had resumed walking the pastures and the creek bottoms of his beloved Vallew, as if nothing deadly and insidious was growing inside of him.

Realizing this might well be his last Christmas, we made plans to spend it with him and his wife, Hildegarde, at their home in Texas. Brenda's sister and her husband joined us and we had a wonderful time together. We looked at old photographs and reminisced late into the night, reliving the good times we had shared at Vallew over the years.

About ten years before retirement, Ben had purchased a piece of property in

East Texas which he christened "Vallew." He built a small, one-room cabin and almost immediately we developed a family tradition of spending holidays there. Brenda's sister, her husband, and their son, would join us. In a fit of holiday madness, all eight of us would crowd into that one room, which served as kitchen, living room, and bedroom. Not infrequently both grandkids, Leah and Scott, would invite a friend, bringing the total occupants to ten.

The overcrowding, and the inconvenience of sleeping on the floor, was far outweighed by the camaraderie we enjoyed. A small wood-burning stove was the only source of heat and the crackling of the fire gave that noisy room a friendly feel. Our only entertainment was what we could provide for ourselves. Consequently, we spent the long evenings playing board games, singing songs, and swapping family stories. It was there that Leah and Scott learned about the Great Depression, about life in the 40's during World War II with its shortages and ration cards, and about Ben and Hildegard's courtship.

My favorite time was early each morning when Ben would slip out of bed and tug on his boots and a jacket. Well do I remember snuggling beneath my warm covers, listening to the small sounds he made as he stirred up the fire and got the coffee maker going. Soon the rich aroma of fresh brewed coffee mingled with the smell of wood smoke coaxing me fully awake. After hastily dressing, I would join him at the table where we sipped coffee and shared conversation as the cabin warmed up, while around us the rest of the family slept peacefully.

After retirement Ben turned that cabin into a lovely three bedroom home with two full baths, and, of all things, a dishwasher. The additional space provided a measure of comfort that the smaller cabin lacked but something was lost, as well. Change is inevitable and probably for the better, still, I would love to have one more Thanksgiving in that crowded cabin; one more Christmas with all the children underfoot.

These and a hundred other thoughts kept me awake long after everyone else had gone to bed on Ben's last Christmas Eve. Staring into the dark, I found myself

thinking of Ben Roy and the good times
we had shared. The memories we made
in those early years at Vallew were rare
and now that special time was gone
forever. Soon Ben would be gone too, and
when he died we would lose not only a
father, but a piece of life we could never
recover. Try as I might, I couldn't help
feeling sad.

Pushing those depressing thoughts to
the back of my mind, I relived the
evening's early festivities. We had deter-
mined to make Ben's last Christmas the
best ever and on Christmas Eve the six of
us celebrated Holy Communion,
marveling anew at the miracle of God's
grace and the hope of eternal life. Then
we exchanged gifts and took a barrage of
pictures. We laughed, sang carols, and cut

up with one another late into the night, but nothing could long banish the looming shadow of death. It tainted everything we did.

January and February passed uneventfully; although Ben Roy continued to lose weight and his strength seemed to be waning. In early March, the doctor informed him that the cancer had spread to his liver and that he probably had only six to eight weeks to live. After careful consideration, Ben decided to spend his last days at home, assisted by hospice care and surrounded by his family. Once that was decided, Leah (our grown daughter) went to Texas to help care for her grandfather.

Brenda and I drove down ten days later so Leah could return home to her family. With the help of hospice, Brenda and her sister cared for their father around the clock for the next four weeks. Of course Hildegarde never left Ben Roy's side. Although he was in excruciating pain, terribly nauseated, and could eat almost nothing he insisted on getting dressed each day. Early on he either sat in the living room or on the deck overlooking the pasture. But as the days passed he grew weaker and he began spending more and more time in bed.

I was only able to stay for a week before resuming a demanding speaking schedule. Telling Ben good-bye was one of the hardest things I've ever done. He was more than just a father-in-law to me. He was one of my dearest friends. Kneeling before him, I took his hands in mine and a host of memories over-whelmed me.

When I was just seventeen-years-old and already dating Brenda, I bought my first car—a 1960 Ford Starliner. It was a bright red, two-door hardtop; beautiful in every way except for the hubcaps. They were just plain ugly. Apparently, Ben felt the same way, because a few days later he presented me with a set of beautiful spinner wheel covers.

Later that summer, my Grandma Miller passed away. Since my parents were in Colorado caring for her, it fell Ben's lot to break the news to me. After telling me she had died, I remember how he stood there, not saying anything, while silent tears ran down my cheeks. The strength I drew from his presence is something I remember to this day.

After Brenda and I married, Ben and I became best friends. He helped me build bookcases and remodel every parsonage in which we lived; often spending his entire vacation working with me. Under his tutelage I learned the art of building and the craft of woodworking—lessons I treasure to this day.

Of course it wasn't all work—we usually found some time to play. Shortly after we moved to Craig, Colorado, in 1975, Ben and Hildegarde came to visit us in early September. With just a hint of fall in the air, I decided it was the perfect time to introduce a South Texan to the joys of trout fishing. I outfitted Ben Roy with waders, a canvas creel, a fishing hat, and a light rod. After a forty-minute drive we parked the car in the shade of some cottonwood trees and headed across a hay meadow toward the William's Fork River.

Reaching the river I selected a shiny gold spinner and tied it on Ben's line. Once I was rigged up we stepped into the swiftly moving water and made our way upstream. Coming to a bend in the river I motioned for Ben to cast into the deeper water near the bank. Moving further upstream I cast my lure into another hole. Over the roar of the river I heard Ben holler, "I got one!" His rod was bent nearly double and I watched as a fourteen-inch rainbow did a tail dance on top of the water.

It took us less than two hours to catch our limit and as we made our way downstream toward the car, I couldn't help thinking that as good as the fishing was the best was yet to come. Just that morning a generous parishioner had delivered a box of large, field-ripened tomatoes to the parsonage. As we were heading out the door to go fishing, Brenda gave me a plastic bag filled with a half dozen of those big red hunkers. Earlier, I had found a sheltered spot and submerged them in the river so they would be good and cold when we returned.

It doesn't get hot in the Rockies like it does in South Texas, but by the time Ben and I got back to where we had left the tomatoes we were hot enough and more than a little sunburned. Retrieving the plastic bag, I handed Ben a chilled tomato and took one for myself. Taking a big bite, my taste buds exploded. Tomato juice sprinkled with little yellow seeds ran down my chin. I looked over at Ben who was enjoying the same messy pleasure. We both grinned, realizing intuitively that life doesn't get any better than that—good fellowship, good fishing, and good tomatoes!

Forcing myself to focus on the present, I turned my attention back to Ben. Tears were clouding my vision and I found it nearly impossible to speak. Sensing my dilemma, he spoke in a voice husky with emotion. "You had best be on your way," he said. "God's work waits on no man and I don't want you lingering here when there's Kingdom work to be done. And don't be canceling any preaching engagements to preach my funeral. If need be, they can hold my body for a few days until you get here. Remember Jesus said, "'...*Let the dead bury their own dead, but you go and proclaim the kingdom of God.*'"[5]

Pulling me close he covered my face and head with kisses. I wanted to speak but I couldn't. I wanted to thank him for all he had done for me and tell him how much I loved him, but the words caught in my throat. I clung to him tenaciously, wanting to believe that I could keep death at bay just by the strength of my will, but of course I couldn't. At last, I loosed my grip and he held me at arms length, looking me full in the face. "I love you Richard," he said, his voice thick with feeling. Choking up, he stumbled to a stop, as salty tears slid down his weathered cheeks. With an effort he regained his composure. "I'll see you on the other side." Releasing me he turned toward the window.

I lurched across the room, nearly blind with grief. At the door, I paused and looked back one last time. Ben was staring out the window at something only he could see, his face bathed in peace. "God be with you, Ben," I croaked, my voice cracking. "You have been a father to me and a friend. I'm going to miss you."

Although Ben lived for three more weeks I never saw him again. With his blessing I resumed my busy speaking schedule, traveling to Arkansas, North Carolina, and New York. I telephoned Brenda everyday, sometimes three and four times a day. She kept me informed regarding Ben's condition. Unfortunately, he suffered terribly and Brenda suffered with him, grieved by her inability to make his dying easier. When death finally overcame him, in the early morning hours on April 21, 2005, it was a relief. At last he was free from this vale of tears. Never again would he writhe in the agony of cancer's slow death. But for those of us who loved him the agony was far from over.

Chapter 2

THE JOURNEY BEGINS

In the immediate aftermath of Ben Roy's death it felt as if we were swathed in great bands of cotton. Life went on, but in slow motion. We continued to comprehend reality and interact with the world, but as if from a great distance. Everything seemed to be filtered through layers and layers of insulation. Looking back, I realize that this was God's way of helping us endure the unendurable. Without it, I don't think any of us could bear the loss of a loved one, the pain would simply be too great.

We were further distanced from the
magnitude of our loss those first few days
by the myriad of details that demanded
our attention. Telephone calls had to be
placed, family and friends informed of
Ben's death. Funeral arrangements had to
be made, the service planned, and flowers
purchased. The house at Vallew was a
beehive of activity. The telephone rang
constantly. Friends were continually drop-
ping by to bring food and express their
condolences. Although we had little interest in conversation and no energy for
fellowshipping, we still found comfort in
being surrounded by caring people.

As a pastor for more than twenty-five
years, I was often amazed at the strength
grieving people seemed to find when I
was present. Now I was experiencing the

same encouragement. The smallest kind-
nesses—an encouraging word, the touch
of a hand on my shoulder, or just the
presence of a friend took on a signifi-
cance heretofore unimagined. In their
presence, I experienced an inner
strengthening I would be hard pressed to
explain. Our circumstances were just as
grim, but somehow they didn't seem as
dark or foreboding.

Of course time waits for no one, and
all too soon the funeral was over and the
last of the family and friends bid us good-
bye to return home. For them the worst
was over, but for us the grief was just
beginning. In their wake the house grew
eerily quiet and without the distraction of
the funeral arrangements and all the other

details, the reality of our loss was finally setting in.

Although my grief was painfully real it was nothing compared to what Brenda and her mother were experiencing. For Hildegarde the loss was unspeakable. After being married to Ben for almost sixty-one years she suddenly found herself alone. Try as she might she couldn't imagine living without him. She had devoted her life to loving him—cooking his favorite foods, ironing his shirts, keeping his house, even styling her hair the way he liked it, and wearing the clothes that pleased him. She felt disoriented and well she might, for without Ben, her world had become unnaturally empty.

Since she would be living alone she decided to close off the two bedrooms upstairs. Of course this necessitated a rearrangement of closets and bathrooms. Although she and Ben had shared a bedroom on the second floor, his closet was off the downstairs bedroom as was the bathroom where he kept his shaving gear and other toiletries. Even though the rearrangement was her idea, emptying Ben's closet was nearly more than she could bear. She asked us to give her a little time and we watched in painful silence as she spent several minutes in the closet touching his clothes. It was, I think, her way of telling him good-bye. Finally, she moved to the bed where she sat mute with grief as we emptied his closet. To this day, she has no memory of moving her things into the bathroom that had always been the one Ben used.

Exhausted though she was, Hildegarde couldn't sleep except in short snatches. She hardly ate at all; the tastiest food was tasteless to her and caught in her throat when she tried to force herself to swallow. Simple tasks felt overwhelming and she seemed to lose interest in the things that once brought her such joy. I had to turn away to hide my tears when she told me that she didn't care whether she cleaned house or not. Although she had always been an immaculate house keeper, she said it didn't matter now; the one she had always done it for wasn't there to appreciate it. What difference did it make whether the house was clean or not?

Watching her wander aimlessly though the house Ben had built for them made my heart hurt. I wanted to do something to ease her pain but what could I do? Anything I might have said would have sounded trite. The thing I realized in that moment was that death is so final. Other tragedies can be overcome but there is nothing you can do about death, no way it can be undone.

And as the weeks passed it didn't seem to get any easier. She loved her home at Vallew but it was hard for her to stay there. Everywhere she turned something would remind her of Ben and with the memory there came a fresh wave of grief. Sitting on the deck, once a relaxing pastime that they enjoyed together, now made her ache with loneliness. The yard with its flower beds and towering oak trees, in times past a source of pride for both of them, now seemed overwhelming in its enormity, just one more thing that had to be taken care of. The long evenings that had afforded them so much pleasure, now seemed endless, the house unnaturally quiet in the dark.

She couldn't walk past the tool shed without seeing his power tools—a planer, a band saw, and a table saw. These very tools were the ones he had used to build their house. Now they sat silent, rusting in the East Texas humidity; powerless without Ben's expertise. The Chevrolet pickup with its turbo diesel engine, duramax transmission, and dual rear wheels was gone, as was the camp trailer Ben pulled with it. The empty carport was just another reminder of how things had changed. Never again would they hook up the trailer and head for Lake Livingston to spend a week camping with their grandson, Scott, and and his wife, Mel. Never again, would they go to Waelder to spend a few days with Uncle Bill and Aunt Dotsie. Never again….

Everywhere Hildegarde looked she saw Ben, only it wasn't him. It was just a shadow; a painful reminder of what once was but would never be again.

Her desolation reminded me of a telephone call I received from a family friend following the death of her husband. He had lost a two-year battle with cancer, leaving her a widow with three children to rear alone. She had held up amazingly well, for the most part, but as the months passed it seemed to her that things were getting worse rather than better. She told me that instead of subsiding, her grief seemed to be intensifying.

I wasn't surprised by the intensity of her feelings. After all, recovering from the death of a spouse often takes up to three years, sometimes longer. Added to her grief was the responsibility of being a single parent. For the first time in her life, she was both the breadwinner and home-maker. Now she had no one to help her with household chores or to share the mundane details involved in managing a family of four. Not only was she respon-sible for cooking, cleaning, and laundry, as well as, child rearing, but she also had to service the cars, take care of the yard, pay the bills, and reconcile the check-book. On top of all of that her job was extremely stressful.

"The thing I hate most," she said, confiding in me, "is that I am becoming such a negative person."

"What do you mean?" I asked.

"It's hard to put into words," she replied. "I guess I'm just tired of living."

Without giving me a chance to respond she plunged ahead. "Don't panic, I'm not suicidal. I could never do that to my children. I'm just tired. All the joy has gone out of my life. There's no color, no sunshine. Everything is a dirty gray."

"The things that once gave me pleasure—walking on the beach, tending my flower garden, and reading to the children—

no longer interest me. Now all I want to do is sleep, but no matter how much sleep I get, I'm always tired."

"It takes a lot of energy to grieve," I offered.

"The worst part," she continued, "is that I don't think it is ever going to end. If I were to be totally honest with myself I would have to say that I've lost all hope of ever being happy again. For me, the future is a black hole."

Looking back on that telephone call, I think I responded with sensitivity and compassion, but now I realize that I didn't have a clue how bad she was hurting. How could I, since I had never lost a spouse? I do know that losing Ben Roy, and trying to comfort Hildegarde and

Brenda during their grief, has given me a greater appreciation for the debilitating power of grief, although I am still mostly ignorant of the depth of our friend's grief and also of Hildegarde's, having never lost a spouse myself.

It seems to me that what makes losing a loved one so hard is the finality of death. There is nothing we can do to rescind it. When a loved one dies, or is killed, there is absolutely nothing we can do to bring them back. We are utterly powerless to undo what is already done. If we are not careful that sense of power-lessness will give way to a numbing hope-lessness. Grief will tempt us to despair, to conclude that life will never be worth living again.

Thinking about it now I find myself remembering a scene from Charles Dickens's classic novel, *Great Expectations*. The last time I read it I was just a sophomore at South Houston High School and far too immature to appreciate its timeless wisdom. Still, these many years later I am reminded of how Dickens captured the essence of despair, a feeling Hildegarde battles every waking moment.

Leaving my computer, I make my way to the bookcases where I keep the classics. After locating *Great Expectations*, I open it and scan the pages until I find the appropriate passage. According to Dickens, all the clocks at Satis House were stopped at 8:40 A.M. At that precise moment, life for Miss Havisham came to a screeching halt. Though she was to live to a ripe old age, her life "stopped" when the villainous Compeyson deserted her at the altar on their wedding day. The woman she once was died. She was put to death, according to Miss Havisham's thinking, by the treachery of the faithless groom. In her place there lived a bitter recluse.

Lest she forget her mistreatment at his hands, Miss Havisham insisted that everything in Satis House remain just the way it was that fateful day. In the far corner of the great hall, where the wedding was to be held, there sat an ancient wedding cake. After many years, it was spotted with mold and draped with many tiers of dusty cobwebs; a pathetic reminder of what might have been, as was Miss Havisham herself. Attired in her original wedding gown, now yellow with age, she roamed the decadent rooms of the once proud Satis House, infecting all who would listen with her bitterness.

Yet it wasn't Compeyson's treacherous act that turned Miss Havisham into a bitter recluse—she did that to herself. And it's a temptation we all face when grief turns into despair. But no matter how bad we are hurting we still have a choice. We can hug our hurts and make a shrine out of our sorrow or we can give our grief to God and embrace life, even though we may not have any interest in it at the time.

In the ensuing weeks I watched Hildegarde fight this battle on many fronts. Even when she forced herself to get on with life it hardly seemed worth it.

Relationships and activities that once brought her so much pleasure now seemed dull and uninteresting. The Scriptures, once a source of encouragement and wisdom, now seemed like just so many words on a page. Prayer often felt like a waste of time and worship was empty at best, unfulfilling. Although both she and Ben were committed Christians and active in their church, going to church now offered little comfort. They had always worshipped together; now the empty space on the pew beside her was just another reminder that Ben was gone and that he was never coming back.

To her credit Hildegarde has not succumbed, she has not allowed herself to withdraw from life. Instead, she has clung tenuously to the spiritual habits of a lifetime and little by little they are restoring her joy and giving her life meaning once again, as they have for countless others.

There's much about grieving that I don't understand, maybe I never will, but one thing I do know—grief itself is not a fatal wound. It's the hurtful things we do to ourselves following the death of a loved one that will do us in. It's the bitterness that kills, or the despair, but never the grief. Given time our hearts will heal themselves. That's the way God made us, at least that's how it seems to me.

Chapter 3

TEMPTATIONS ALONG THE WAY

Grieving, as I'm sure you know, is hard work and fraught with numerous snares such as anger and guilt. These powerful emotions can undermine grief's healing work, causing us to waste valuable time and energy. That is not to say we shouldn't feel these things, in fact almost everyone has to contend with them to some degree, but we must be careful not to get stuck there.

Both Hildegarde and Brenda were tempted with varying degrees of anger although for decidedly different reasons.

Hildegarde's anger was largely directed at the doctor. Not the surgeon who removed the cancerous tumor from Ben's colon but the doctor who first discovered the polyps. Although he encouraged Ben to have them removed as a precautionary measure, he did not clearly identify the risk of cancer if they were not taken out. To Hildegarde's way of thinking that made him at least partially responsible for Ben's death. He should have emphatically stated the risk and insisted that Ben have those polyps removed!

Although she knew it was pointless she could not help falling into the "If only…" trap from time to time. If only the doctor had been more insistent. If only Ben had not been so adamant about not returning for the second treatment. If only she had encouraged him to have all of the polyps removed. If only….

Instead of being angry with the doctor, Brenda blamed herself. When her father discussed his decision to not have the remaining polyps removed with us, she remembers encouraging him to ignore the doctor's advice. My recollection of that conversation is slightly different. I remember that Brenda and I both encouraged Ben to do what he felt was right for him. In retrospect I wish we had done differently. I wish we had done some serious research so we could have offered Ben more informed advice, but we didn't.

It would be easy to get stuck there— to rage at the doctor or to blame ourselves—but it's pointless. Nothing we do now will bring Ben back. Neither anger, nor blame, nor regret can reverse what has happened, so it behooves us to release these negative emotions—not repress them—and move on. This is a choice, an act of our will. It is not easy but with God's help we can do it.

Experience has taught me that in times of great grief our emotions are often misdirected, although we may not be consciously aware of it. Sure we blame the doctor but ultimately medical science can only do so much and we all know that. Yes, we wish we had done things differently and we do feel a certain responsibility, even guilt. Maybe if we had insisted, Ben might have had those polyps removed and never been stricken with cancer, but we don't know that. It might have changed nothing.

But beneath all of these surface issues lies a deeper one; one I am almost afraid to acknowledge. While we may rage at the doctors or even second-guess ourselves, ultimately it is God we hold responsible. Although I never admitted my feelings to anyone, in my heart I was disappointed with God. I felt He had let us down. He could have intervened on Ben's behalf—either prevented his illness or healed him—but it seemed He did nothing and that's what hurt the most. I love God and it troubles me to feel this way, but I can't deny that I have moments when I feel deeply disappointed, even angry with Him. I *know* He is too wise to ever make a mistake and too loving to ever cause one of His children needless pain and yet that doesn't keep me from *feeling* like He let us down.

In times like this I am reminded of the man who suffered a crisis of belief in the story of Dovid Din of Jerusalem from *The Hasidic Tales.* No matter what counsel Reb Dovid offered, the man dismissed it. So Reb Dovid decided to say nothing, just listen. For hours the man ranted and raved. Finally, Reb Dovid asked, "Why are you so angry with God?"

This question stunned the man, as he had said nothing at all about God. He grew very quiet and looked at Dovid Din and said: "All my life I have been so afraid to express my anger to God that I have always directed my anger at people who are connected with God. But until this moment I did not understand this."[6]

According to the story Reb Dovid led the man to the Wailing Wall. Not to the place where people pray but to the site of the ruins of the Temple. When they reached that place, Reb Dovid told him that it was time to express all the anger he felt toward God. For more than an hour, the man struck the wall of the *Kotel* and screamed his heart out. Then he began to cry and could not stop crying. Little by little his cries became sobs that turned into prayers.

Isn't that what happens when we take our hardest questions, our honest doubts, and even our inexplicable anger to God? I think so. The Holy Spirit turns our grief, even our anger into prayer.

Consider the emotional exchange Mary and Martha had with Jesus following the death of their brother. When Lazarus fell sick his sisters immediately sent for Jesus[7] but He tarried two more days before setting out for Bethany. By the time He finally arrived Lazarus was four days dead.[8]

Four days!

Four days for Mary and Martha to stew about what might have been. Four days for them to remember the many times Jesus had enjoyed their hospitality, the good times they had shared. Four days to wonder if His friendship was just a sham, just a ploy to take advantage of

their kindness and generosity. It broke
Mary's heart but it made Martha angry
and when Jesus finally arrived in Bethany
she stormed out to meet Him. *"Lord,"*
she fumed, *"if you had been here, my
brother would not have died."*[9]

Angrily Martha accused Jesus of
failing, of not caring, of ignoring them in
the hour of their greatest need. That's
how she *felt* but on a deeper level she
knew better. Even in her grief and anger
she still trusted Him. And once she had
expressed her feelings, faith found its
voice, *"'…I believe that you are the
Christ, the Son of God, who was to come
into the world.'"*[10] *"'I know he [Lazarus]
will rise again in the resurrection at the
last day….'"*[11]

What did Jesus do? How did He respond to Martha? He absorbed her anger without rebuke. He understood how things must seem from her limited perspective, how much she loved her brother, and how deeply she hurt. And when she suddenly moved from anger to faith Jesus moved with her and built on her confession. He said to her, *"…'I am the resurrection and the life. He who believes in me will live, even though he dies; and whoever lives and believes in me will never die.'"*[12]

Mary responded differently—illustrating how two people can grieve the same tragedy in decidedly different ways. She was more hurt than angry in keeping with her temperament, weeping instead of raging, her tears at least as accusing as Martha's temper.

"*When Mary reached the place where Jesus was and saw him, she fell at his feet and said, `Lord, if you had been here, my brother would not have died.'*"

"*When Jesus saw her weeping…he was deeply moved in spirit and troubled…[and] Jesus wept.*"[13]

For Mary, Jesus had no theological pronouncements, no revelation about resurrection life, and no discourse about His divine Sonship. Why? Not because they were any less true now, but because Mary was not ready to receive them. There was little or no faith in her confession, beyond the faith to tell Jesus how she really felt. Somehow, even in her grief and disappointment, she believed He would understand, and He did. **He wept with her.** He embraced her grief, made her sorrow His own. He was truly touched by the feelings of her infirmities.[14]

During the difficult days following Ben's death this passage in John and the truths gleaned from it became a source of strength for me. Like Mary and Martha, I had mixed emotions, and I think Brenda and Hildegarde did too. In our heart of hearts we trusted God and nothing was going to change that. Still there were moments when our grief was so great that we railed at God—"Lord You could have healed Ben Roy but You didn't. All You had to do was speak the word and we could have been spared this unspeakable loss."

In those times, I took great comfort in knowing God could handle my wildly vacillating emotions. There were times when I was tempted to pretend I had it all together, that I wasn't struggling. But I also knew that if I repressed my feelings they would poison my spirit. The only cure was to honestly confess them to God. If He absorbed Martha's anger without rebuking her then surely He would not reject me. Surely, He understood my pain and the questions it birthed.[15]

As contradictory as it seems, expressing our hurt and disappointment, even our anger to God, is not an act of rebellion but rather an act of worship. By verbalizing our *real* feelings rather than simply saying *right* things, we offer our brokenness[16] and sorrow, even our humanness, as gifts to a God we trust even if we can't always understand His ways. And neither is the enormity of our grief a negative reflection on our faith, rather it is evidence of our profound loss and the depth of the love we shared with the departed.

While Hildegarde struggled with the loss caused by Ben's death and the nagging questions about why God hadn't healed him, the thing that bothered Brenda the most was the manner in which her father had died. She could accept his death and rejoice in the knowledge that he was alive with Christ, but she couldn't understand why he had to suffer so and why his death had been so painfully hard.

The cancer that had begun in Ben's colon soon spread to his liver and in early March the doctor informed us that he would probably live no more than six to eight weeks. We continued to pray for his healing but Ben seemed at peace with whatever the future held. On more than one occasion he said, "If Heaven is all the Bible says it is then why do we cling to this life so desperately? I've had a full life and if this is my time I'm ready to go and be with the Lord."

Medically speaking Ben had little or no hope, so with the help of hospice we prepared to make his last days as comfortable as possible. We set up a hospital bed in the downstairs bedroom where he could look out the window and see his beloved Vallew, as spring turned the trees and pastures a vibrant green. Unfortunately, he wasn't able to take much pleasure in the coming of spring with its gentle days and lingering light. His illness was ruthless, soon reducing his world to a prison of pain. He had a few reasonably good days but for the most part he suffered unspeakably.

The last three weeks of his life were unbearably hard. He was so nauseated he could eat nothing and soon even the faintest smell of food caused him to gag and throw up. The anti-nausea medicine prescribed by the doctor was largely ineffective; reducing somewhat the number of times Ben vomited but never eliminating his nausea. To complicate matters, after taking it he would become extremely agitated and see things in the room that were not there. He hated that feeling and with increasing frequency Brenda found herself having to choose between his unbearable nausea and hallucination. No matter what she chose—to give him the medicine or to withhold it—her father suffered terribly and she suffered with him, hating her inability to make his last days easier.

In an attempt to give him some relief, the doctor continued to increase the dosage, but to no avail. Finally, he directed the hospice nurse to give Ben the medicine by injection. She had hardly left the house before he reacted to the injection. One minute he was conscious, responding to Brenda and her mother, the next minute he was unconscious. For several minutes it looked like he was going to die before he finally regained consciousness. When he did it was apparent that he had suffered a small stroke. It left one side of his face partially paralyzed giving him a crooked smile and making it impossible for him to close one eye. He bore it all with remarkably good humor and even managed to straighten his lopsided grin by holding up one side of his mouth with his finger.

But even his good humor could not keep the cancer at bay. Day by day his pain intensified, moderated the last few days by ever increasing amounts of morphine. For more than twenty-four hours, Brenda sat beside his bed giving him morphine every fifteen minutes, per the doctor's instructions. Exhausted, she finally asked the hospice nurse if there was some way to adjust the machine that dispensed the

morphine so she would not have to acti-
vate it manually. The hospice nurse
assured her there was and she proceeded
to reset the machine before leaving.

The weight of caring for her father was
a burden Brenda could not put down day
or night, not for a single minute, and by
now she was ready to collapse. Wearily,
she sank into a chair beside his bed and
fell into restless sleep. A short time later
she was jerked awake when her father sat
up in bed and screamed. His face was
contorted in agony, his entire body jerking
in pain. Since it appeared the morphine
was not strong enough to control his pain,
Brenda called me on the telephone and
asked me to pray. For more than an hour I
interceded, imploring God for relief, while
she held the phone next to her father's ear.

My prayers seemed to bring Ben a measure of comfort but they did little or nothing to ease his horrific pain. Finally, I bid Brenda good-bye so she could call hospice. When the nurse arrived she discovered the machine was malfunctioning. No wonder Ben was in agony. He wasn't getting any morphine. Even though they eventually got it working, after a sort, it was too late to help him. By then his pain was raging out of control and the limited amounts of morphine dispensed by the malfunctioning machine did almost nothing to relieve his agony. Hours later the endless night finally drew to a close, and as the first fingers of light touched the sky Ben breathed his last. Hildegarde was holding his hand when he died, and as his trembling body grew still, she whispered, "He's gone."

Relieved as she was that her father's suffering was over, Brenda was tormented with both anger and regret. Although she was too gracious to express her feelings, on the inside she raged at what she considered the incompetence of the hospice workers. Only when it was too late did they suggest giving Ben morphine intravenously. What were they thinking? Didn't they care? And she blamed herself for not being able to do more. She should have been more assertive. She should have taken the initiative in directing his care, never mind that she had no medical training.

No matter how hard she had tried, she had not been able to save her father from

the excruciating pain that accompanied
his death. For months afterward, she
struggled with feelings of failure. She felt
she had let him down, that she should
have been able to do more to make his
dying easier. And she felt God had let her
down. To her way of thinking, if her
father had to die, the least God could do
was let him die in peace. But no matter
how hard she had prayed nothing
changed, and in the days and weeks
following the funeral she found herself
tormented by memories of the way he
died. This made it nearly impossible for
her to remember the rich life he had lived
or to celebrate the promise of eternal life.
She knew these things were true but her
grief rendered them unreal, robbing them
of their power to comfort.

Chapter 4

THE POWER OF HIS PRESENCE

The thing we learned through all of this is that there are no answers; at least there are no answers that can take our hurt away. There were theological explanations, to be sure, scripturally accurate, detailing the doctrine of sin and death, as well as the promise of eternal life. Yet these theological truths did not answer the "why" questions—Why is one child taken in infancy and not another? Why is a good man stricken in the prime of life while an ungodly man lives to a ripe old age? Why did Ben Roy have to die? Why? Why? Why? Even if we could have figured out the "why" it would not have changed a thing—not the fact of Ben's death or the pain of our loss.

Suffice it to say that we inhabit a planet that is in rebellion and that we are part of a race living outside of God's will. One consequence of that rebellion is sickness and death.[17] As believers our sins have been forgiven,[18] we are new creations in Christ,[19] yet we remain a part of this human family—a family that is tainted by sin and death. As a result, we too suffer the inevitable repercussions of that fallen state—i.e. sickness and death. Beyond that, the "why" of a particular death will remain a mystery known only to God. But of one thing I am sure—God is not to blame. When tragedy strikes, when a loved one dies, God's heart is the first of all hearts to break.

Thinking about all of this now, I am reminded of the two despairing disciples on the road to Emmaus. With high hopes, they had set out for Jerusalem to celebrate the Passover. As followers of Jesus, they were hopeful that He might reveal Himself as the promised Messiah. Instead, to their dismay, He was betrayed by one of His own, falsely condemned by the Sanhedrin, and unjustly executed by the Romans. And when Jesus died their hopes and dreams died with Him.

The incredible miracles that Jesus had done, the wonderful things he had taught, remained unchanged but now their grief rendered them unreal. The memories of the wonderful times they had shared with Jesus were lost in the horror of His death,

swallowed up in the sorrow that threat-
ened to consume them.

Even when Jesus Himself joined them
along the way they did not recognize
Him. Blinded by their grief, they simply
assumed He was just another weary
pilgrim returning home. Even when He
expounded the Scriptures to them,
proving that the crucifixion was not a
colossal mistake but a vital part of God's
eternal plan, they could not be comforted.

Based on their experience, and my
own, I can only conclude that "answers"
alone are no match for grief. Answers are
important, to be sure, but not without
relationship. The eternal truths Jesus
taught them as they journeyed to Emmaus
became "real" only when He revealed

Himself to them in the breaking of
bread[20]—that is in relationship. Then and
only then did their grief give way to
joyous hope. In stunned amazement they
asked each other, *Were not our hearts
burning within us while he talked with us on
the road, and opened the scriptures to us?*[21]

When I was just a boy of eight or nine,
we lived in a green house, situated beneath
towering Elm trees, on Chestnut Street in
Sterling, Colorado. Although Sterling's
population numbered less than 10,000
people, it was the county seat and the largest
town in a radius of nearly one hundred
miles. Much to the chagrin of the town
fathers, Sterling suffered a series of burgla-
ries. Almost weekly another home would
be burglarized and the police had made no
arrests. In fact, they seemed clueless.

One evening, just before bedtime, I overheard dad and mom discussing the latest incident. Needless to say the situation was making them uncomfortable, as it was most families. I went to bed thinking about these things and awoke shortly after midnight to see a man rummaging through the things in my closet. I tried to scream but I couldn't make a sound. Fear's bony hand squeezed my throat shut, making me mute. For thirty seconds, a minute, maybe more, I couldn't do anything. I lay there frozen with fear. Finally, I managed a blood-curdling scream, and my father came charging into my bedroom. Of course, the intruder vanished and after a time Dad managed to calm my fears and I was finally able to go back to sleep.

Some time later I awoke again and the intruder was back; in fact he was standing right beside my bed. I lay there trying not to breath, more afraid than I've ever been before or since. I knew I had to do something but I was afraid to move. With a sudden lunge, I sat straight up in bed and screamed loud enough to wake the dead. In an instant, Dad burst into the room, baseball bat in hand. Again, the intruder disappeared.

Of course, now that I'm older I realize that intruder was most likely just a figment of my overactive imagination, but you couldn't have convinced me of that back then. In fact, after the second experience, I refused to be comforted. My father's exhortations fell on deaf ears. It didn't matter that he had checked all the doors and windows and found them securely locked. It made no difference that he had gone through the house room by room without finding anything amiss. I would not be comforted. Finally, in desperation, he sent my younger brother to sleep with my mother and he climbed into bed beside me. When he did, my fear fled!

What answers, and assurances, and exhortations could not do, my father's presence did. He comforted me. As long as he was with me I had no fear.

That is what the Psalmist is talking about when he writes:

> *"Even though I walk*
> *through the valley of the*
> *shadow of death,*
> **I will fear no evil,**

> *for you are with me;*
> *your rod and your staff,*
> *they comfort me."*[22]

It wasn't answers or theological truths that comforted the psalmist; it was the Shepherd's presence! In fact the Shepherd's presence[23] makes answers unnecessary, replacing understanding with something far better—unconditional trust. Of course, His presence does not eliminate our grief—nothing can do that—but it does put it into eternal perspective and through our tears we declare, *"…'Death has been swallowed up in victory.'"*[24]

Years ago, I was passing through a particularly difficult time—grieving, not the death of a loved one, but the death of a cherished dream. One night I couldn't sleep, so troubled was my mind. In the wee hours of the morning I slipped out of bed and made my way into the living room, being careful to make no noise. Moonlight was streaming through the bay window as I stretched out on the window seat and stared at the darkness beyond the glass.

I prayed silently for several minutes, grieving the foolish decisions I had made over the past months. Those very decisions had precipitated several painful rejections, created a financial crisis, and caused me to doubt myself. In my depression I was tormented with the thought that there would never be a place for me in ministry again. At a deeper level I found myself wondering if God still loved me. Intellectually, I knew God's love was unconditional, based on who He is and not on anything I had or had not done, yet on an emotional level I felt completely alone, abandoned by God.

Silent tears slid down my cheeks and in my heart I cried out, *Do you love me, God? Do you still love me?*

In that instant my eighteen-month-old daughter climbed onto the window seat and straddled my bare chest. Placing her chubby little hands on my tear dampened cheeks she said, "I luv you, Daddy. I luv you."

It was her voice I heard and it was her hands I felt on my face, but it was God who spoke to me, of that I have absolutely no doubt!

As I think about it now, these many years later, I can't help but wonder what

woke her and why she didn't cry out.
How did she get out of bed without
waking her mother? How did she find her
way through the house in the dark, and
why wasn't she afraid? I can only
conclude that God brought her to me. He
spoke to me through her, using her little
voice to assure me of His great love.

At other times the Father's presence is
so real that we don't need anything else—
not special people or special places. But
those experiences are rare, and more often
than not God manifests His presence
through others. In my case, He comforted
me through the words of my baby daughter, Leah Starr. For author Sue Monk
Kidd, it was the kindness of an elderly
gentleman with thinning white hair. Of
that experience she wrote:

Soon after midnight I rose from the tiny, sleepless cot in my husband's hospital room. He lay terribly sick. Beyond the window no moon shone. Not even a street lamp pierced the darkness that churned against the pane. It seemed the night conspired with the darkness in my soul…with the churning anguish I felt over my husband's precarious condition.

As my fears blackened, I pulled on my shoes and fled out into the hospital corridor where dim artificial light laced the wall with shadows. Tears trembled on my face…a sob crowded my throat. A few feet away I saw the visitor's elevator, its door open. I ducked inside and fumbled with the buttons. As it swept me up, my sobs gave way, echoing anonymously along the elevator's silent pathway. I do not know how many times

I rode up and down while my despair poured out. But it was the middle of the night, and who would notice.

Suddenly I heard a soft ping. The elevator stopped. The doors opened. Inside stepped an elderly man with thinning white hair and eyes that searched the tears streaming down my face. He pushed a button, then dug into his pocket. As we lurched upward he handed me a neatly folded handkerchief. I wiped my eyes, staring into his kind, steady gaze. And his compassion reached my heart like the first fingers of morning sun dispelling the night. God was strangely present in the little elevator, as if He were there in the old man's face.

The doors swished open. I thanked the stranger and handed back his handkerchief, damp and soiled with my anguish. Then he nodded me a gentle smile and slipped away.

As I returned to my husband's room, I was quite sure…God does not fail us in our distress. His compassion is everywhere. And the tenderest promise in the Bible is true—God shall wipe away every tear from their eyes.

And He shall…one way or another.[25]

Many grieving people report seeing and/or having conversations with their departed loved ones. Psychologists tend to dismiss these experiences as hallucinations, saying grieving people see things that aren't there, but at least some of them may be spiritual experiences—a dream or a vision—that transcend the limits of our physical world.

For instance, one night, about a year after Ben Roy's death, Hildegarde suddenly awoke sensing someone was in the room with her. Turning she saw Ben standing beside her bed. As she watched he came over and putting his arm around her he pulled her close. Although his nearness was enormously comforting, she knew he couldn't be there. Turning so she could face him she said, "You're not supposed to be here, you're dead."

Ben smiled and said, "You're wrong." And then he was gone.

It is important to note that Hildegarde was not trying to contact Ben nor would she. She may have been hallucinating as the psychologists suggest or possibly dreaming. I tend to think God gave her a dream or even a vision in order to comfort her. Although she believed in eternal life and was convinced that Ben was alive with Christ,[26] she was tormented with thoughts that maybe they wouldn't recognize each other in eternity. Death, she feared, had ended forever the special relationship they had shared for more than sixty years as husband and wife. Not just in this world but also in the world to come.

Earlier she had discussed her concerns with me. The thing that prompted her confusion was the passage of Scripture where Jesus said, *"At the resurrection people will neither marry nor be given in marriage; they will be like the angels in heaven."*[27]

I tried to reassure her by suggesting that Jesus simply meant that in eternity the essence of our relationships would transcend their earthly limits. We would still "know" each other but in a way heretofore unimaginable. I acknowledged that her relationship with Ben would obviously be different but I could not imagine that it would be diminished. Everything about Heaven supersedes everything earthly so why would our relationships be any different?

Opening the Bible, I pointed out that every glimpse the Scriptures give us of people in eternity reveals that they were known and recognized by their earthly identities. On the mount of transfiguration the disciples saw Moses and Elijah conversing with Jesus.[28] The rich man who died recognized both Abraham and Lazarus in eternity.[29]

I think Hildegarde was encouraged but I could tell she still wasn't convinced. When she told Ben, "You're not supposed to be here, you're dead," she was speaking out of her fear. She was telling him that the special relationship they had once known could never be again. To her way of thinking they might live forever but it would never be the same.

To which Ben replied, "You're wrong."

Whatever her experience was—a dream, a vision, or a hallucination—it was the thing God used to ease her concerns. It was a source of great comfort to her; much more so than the logic I employed in our theological discussion. In fact, in the weeks that followed she returned to that experience again and again, drawing strength from it. And like C.S. Lewis, she became convinced that "…the union between the risen spouses will be as close as that between the soul and its own risen body."[30]

Of course this experience did not end her grief but it did give her a renewed hope for the future. There were still times when her pain was nearly unbearable but not as often, nor did they last as long. And frequently, in the midst of them she would experience a remarkable peace; even a certain joy, although it was richly seasoned with tears. During one of those times she found herself humming an original melody and then words started coming to her. Slipping out of bed, she turned on the lamp and rummaged in the nightstand until she found a pen and a sheet of ruled

paper. Blinking back her tears, she began
to write a love song for Ben.

I'm thinking of you,
I'm thinking of you.
Every place that I go,
Every thing that I do,
I'm thinking of you,
I'm thinking of you.

I remember the good times,
I remember the sad,
And I'm so grateful to you
for the love that we had.
I pray it's not over,
In our eternal life to be
I hope when I see you
Your eyes still speak to me.

If I could do it over
More love to you I'd give.
This wish I'll have always

So long as I live.
But to live life over
There's never a chance,
So with our memories
I must advance.

I miss your strong arms
And your sweet, tender kiss,
The sound of your voice
and the sound of your steps.
Here I know it's all over
But eternity I can see.
That is the one thing
So important to me.

I'm thinking of you,
I'm thinking of you.
Every place that I go,
Every thing that I do.
I'm thinking of you,
I'm thinking of you.

Chapter 5

❧

FROM GRIEF TO GRATEFULNESS

Even though Hildegarde was enormously comforted by those experiences she continued to question. To her way of thinking it made no sense that Ben Roy should die. He was a godly man and she needed him. Repeatedly she asked me, "Why would God take Ben and then allow some scoundrel to enjoy good health and a long life?"

Mostly I just listened, offering what comfort I could but not really saying much. When I did reason with her, I pointed out how much she had to be thankful for. She and Ben had enjoyed nearly sixty-one years of marriage, not to mention the fact that Ben had remarkably good health until the last six months of his life. His mind was sharp and he remained active and productive until the very end.

As the months passed, I began to encourage her to offer God a sacrifice of praise. "Give God thanks for the life you shared with Ben," I suggested. "And praise Him for the promise of eternal life when you will be together again."

"Although the ultimate reality of Heaven is beyond our comprehension," I reasoned, "God has revealed the essence of it. And always that essence is of a far grander scale than anything this earthly life affords. That being the case, we know the best is yet to come."

I was talking to myself as much as I was to her. For too long I had been mired in my sorrow, reflecting only on all I had lost when Ben died. With an effort, I turned my thoughts toward the life he had lived; remembering with thankfulness the richness he had brought into my own life and what a special man he had been. Although he had only a tenth grade education, he was one of the wisest men I have ever known. His friends, and even his pastor, considered him a Bible scholar though he insisted he was just a student of the Word. Whether he was a scholar or just a student, one thing was apparent—he lived what he believed. His values were deeply rooted in the truth of Scripture and his life reflected his love for the Lord.

Ben's curiosity was insatiable and he never stopped learning. Computers fascinated him and he taught himself to type and use the Internet after he was seventy-years-old. He had little interest in television beyond the national news and he considered sports a waste of time. For entertainment, he studied the encyclopedia or Webster's dictionary. On more occasions than I like to remember he would ask me if I was sure I was using a particular word correctly. Of course I insisted I was, after all I am a writer and public speaker. Gently he would suggest we look it up in the dictionary. Occasionally, I was right but more often than not, he was.

He loved to discuss what he referred to as "the things of the Lord," and he spent hours researching the Scriptures. Even

when we disagreed he was never argumen-
tative. At his funeral his pastor told of a
discussion he had with Ben regarding
communion. In the course of their conversation he had referred to the bread and the
cup[31] as "symbols" of the Lord's broken
body and shed blood. Ben asked, "Have
you read that passage carefully?" That's all
he said, nothing more. After rereading all
of the passages related to the Lord's
Supper, his pastor said he realized that to
refer to the communion emblems as
"symbols" was to do the words of Jesus an
injustice. What might have precipitated an
argument became an opportunity for
enlightenment because of the gentle way
Ben handled the discussion.

When word of Ben's illness spread
through Tennessee Colony and the

surrounding area, a parade of visitors descended on Vallew. Brenda and I were amazed at the number of people who visited. We knew Ben was loved but we had no idea how wide spread the affection was or in what high esteem the church and community held him. Again and again, people told us how much Ben meant to them. A number of people said, "I don't know what we will do without him. He's a spiritual father to so many of us."

Listening to them simply reaffirmed what we already knew. Ben was a very special man and well loved, and I realized anew how blessed I was to have shared a nearly life-long relationship with him. We were close, closer than a father-in-law and a son-in-law had any right to be, but that doesn't mean we always saw eye to eye.

Although we shared many things in common, we were different in many ways, as well. For instance, I am an avid sports enthusiast while Ben had little or no interest in athletic events. I love to fish. Ben couldn't have cared less. I'm a voracious reader. Ben was not. In fact, in his seventy-eight years he only read one novel—*True Women* by Janice Woods Windle. And the only reason he read it was because he grew up with some of the people mentioned in the last few pages.

So why were Ben and I so close? For one thing, we both loved the same woman—his youngest daughter Brenda, who also happens to be my wife. She was the one who brought us together. I was just a teenager when I began dating her and soon Ben was treating me like the son he never had. He was my first Bible teacher, opening the Scriptures to me week after week as we sat around his dining room table following a Sunday dinner of the best pot roast I have ever put in my mouth. When I entered the ministry he was my most avid supporter and when I asked to marry Brenda he not only gave me his permission but his blessing, as well. Over the years, he provided wise counsel, encouragement, prayer support, and help any time I needed it. He was my friend and I never made a major decision without consulting him.

I knew losing Ben would hurt but I had no idea the huge hole his death would leave in my heart. He's been gone nearly two years now and I still miss him every day. Everywhere I turn I see something that reminds me of him. Early in the morning, when I build a fire in the antique wood-burning stove in our cabin overlooking Beaver Lake, I think of him. As I sip my coffee, I remember all the mornings we enjoyed the warmth of the fire, as we watched the sun chase away the last of the fog laying low above the water. Walking through the woods, as autumn stains the leaves in flaming hues; I remember how much he loved this time of the year. Sitting on the dock as evening falls, I listen to the gentle lapping of the waves and blink back my tears. What I wouldn't give to have just one more chance to share a moment like this with Ben.

Recently, a storm struck and for several hours high winds and heavy rains battered our property, leaving in its wake nearly fifty uprooted trees. Had Ben been living he and I would have cleaned up our six acres but instead I called a commercial company to remove the fallen trees. They cut them into logs six to eight feet long. My plan was to cut and split the logs for firewood as time permitted. Unfortunately, several months have passed and the log piles are still untouched. I haven't cut or split a single one. If Ben were still living I would have a two to three year supply of firewood—cut, split, and neatly stacked. It's not that I can't do it without him, but it seems I always find an excuse not to.

My chain saws need tuned up and the chains need sharpened but I can't bring myself to make the two-hour trek to town. It just seems like too much trouble. If Ben were here that wouldn't be a problem. We would just fill a thermos with coffee and hit the road, relishing the opportunity for a couple of hours of uninterrupted conversation. Back home we would tackle the logs, enjoying the chill in the air and the pungent odor of fresh cut wood. By the day's end we would be tired, our backs aching, but not too tired for a game of forty-two with Brenda and Hildegarde.

Every time Ben came to the cabin he "forced" me to do what I really wanted to do, but never took the time to do. He loved a project and wasn't happy if we weren't working on something—closing in a covered porch or building a deck. I'm ashamed to admit it but since he's been gone I haven't done a single project. It's not that I can't do it without him but somehow it's not the same. Besides, it seems I always have a book to write or a conference to preach.

Thinking about it now I realize that I have been doing Ben's memory a disservice. The way to honor him is not by wallowing in my grief, never daring to do the things we once did together, but to carry on. Of course, I will never be able to repay him for his many investments into my life, but I *can* pass them on. The values and skills he imparted to me can be shared with others—my son-in-law and my grandson, for instance.

In truth, I think the time has come for me to change my focus. Until now I have been obsessed with what I lost when Ben died—a father, a friend, a confidant, and a mentor. Initially, that was appropriate but I think I have reached the point where I need to move on. It's time to stop remembering Ben's death and give thanks to God for the incredible life he lived and the special relationship we shared. In fact, that's the only way to get from grief to gratefulness.

Like most of you, Hildegarde, Brenda, and I were largely ignorant of what lay in store for us when we embarked on this journey through the valley of the shadow of death. Thankfully, we received help along the way. Friends called to encourage us and their faithful prayers sustained us when our strength failed. Others sent cards, letters, and even books. One of the things that helped me most was a small book entitled *Tracks of a Fellow Struggler* by John Claypool. In reference to the death of his ten-year-old daughter, he wrote:

> *I have two alternatives: dwelling on the fact that she has been taken away, I*

can dissolve in remorse that all of this is gone forever, or, focusing on the wonder that she was given to us at all, I can learn to be grateful that we shared life, even for an all-too-short ten years…The way of remorse does not alter the stark reality one whit and only makes matters worse. The way of gratitude does not alleviate the pain, but it somehow puts some light around the darkness and builds strength to begin to move on.[32]

Like John, we all have the same two alternatives—remorse or thanksgiving. For instance, I can dwell on what I lost when Ben died or I can give thanks for what we shared while he lived. The choice is mine. If I choose to dwell only on his death, I risk becoming a tragic figure, not unlike the fictional Miss Havisham in *Great*

Expectations. On the other hand, if I choose to give thanks to God for the experience of sharing in Ben's life, I open my heart to receive healing. That doesn't mean I won't ever grieve again or that I won't miss Ben. Rather it means that not even death can rob me of the special relationship we shared. In truth, even life's tragedies can be a source of spiritual richness if we have faith, and a lifetime of memories to draw upon.

Nearly two years have passed since that April morning when Ben breathed his last breath and much has changed. Just this month Hildegarde has returned to Vallew, to live alone in the house Ben built; having finally grown weary of living out of a suitcase. Although she once thought she would never be able to live in that house without him, she is now back in her own home and at peace.

Yesterday, she called to tell Brenda how much she was enjoying church again and today she helped deliver Christmas baskets to the retirement center. Never mind that she is older than many of the residents who live there.

Looking out my study window, I see that snow covers the ground on this bitterly cold December morning, but not even winter's chill can diminish the gratitude that warms my heart. In worship we have offered our grief to God—what the Bible calls a *sacrifice of praise*[33]—and He is *turning our wailing into dancing.*[34] Well it has been said, "*...weeping may remain for a night, but rejoicing comes in the morning.*"[35]

EPILOGUE

I wrote much of *From Grief to Gratefulness* sitting at a small desk in the corner of the dining room in my sister's home in Friendswood, Texas, while helping care for my ailing father. In early November, 2006, he fell and broke his hip. Subsequently, he underwent surgery and several weeks of rehabilitation before being released to our care. My sister turned the office in her home into a sick room and all of us chipped in to purchase a queen size adjustable bed so mother could continue to sleep with Daddy.

It soon became apparent that Dad was dying although neither my sister nor my mother could bring themselves to admit it. The thought of losing him was simply more than they could bear. As the end drew near, all the children and grandchildren, and even the great-grandchildren gathered at my sister's home.

On Thursday afternoon, February 8, 2007, my father departed this world. His home going was peaceful, although the weeks preceding it were filled with considerable suffering. He bore it all with remarkable grace—the pain and choking, the inability to eat and the humiliation of not being able to care for himself. As the end drew near he became ever more affectionate, repeatedly kissing and hugging those of us who cared for him.

The last Sunday before his death we all crowded around his bed for worship. For the most part Dad seemed oblivious, but when it came time to receive communion he opened his eyes and reached for the cup and the bread. Kneeling beside his bed, I took his hand and began to quote John 14:2,3. As I quoted the familiar words, *"In my Father's house are many mansions…"* he moved his lips, sound-lessly mouthing the words along with me. As we sang his favorite hymns he seemed to draw strength from them. Not strength to live but the strength to pass from this life to the next without fear.

Two days later he fell into a coma from which he awakened only momentar-ily at the very end. Mother was lying on the bed beside him, as was my sister. My brothers were at his bedside. Bob was standing at the head of the bed softly stroking Daddy's hair, while Don was standing beside him holding Daddy's hand. Standing between them and just a little behind, I had a clear view of my Father's face. For days he had laid with his head back and his mouth wide open as he labored to breath, but as he drew his last breath he closed his mouth and opened his eyes. Focusing on something only he could see, Daddy smiled and tried to sit up, and then he was gone.

Thinking about it now, I am sure Jesus came for Dad just as He promised He would, *"…if I go and prepare a place for you, I will come back and take you to be with me that you also may be where I am."*[36] There was no death angel in that room, just the Lord of life coming to call my father to his eternal reward.

The images of the last days I spent with my father have been forever etched upon my heart. One of the many things I will never forget is the memory of the love and devotion heaped upon him by his family and friends. It was a rare and special thing and I can only conclude that the man or woman who goes into eternity loved like that is rich indeed.

The funeral service was deeply moving, filled with memories of the past and hope for the future. No one captured the hope of eternal life more powerfully than my brother Don. Having spent the last thirty years as a missionary serving in Latin America he understands what it means to be a pilgrim and a stranger in a foreign land. When it was his turn to speak he said, "For the past thirty years I have been required to carry official documents identifying me as a 'resident alien.' Although I drink mate like an Argentine, eat asado with the best of them, and speak the language as if it were my mother tongue, I am still a 'resident alien' and I always will be. I love Argentina and its people but I will never be an Argentine. I am an American and America will always be my home."

Pausing to collect himself he continued, "When we went to the mission field in 1976 we were truly cut off from our families and our homeland. There was no satellite television or Internet and it took weeks to arrange an international telephone call, not to mention the prohibitive expense. After four long years we flew home for our first furlough. When we landed at the Miami International Airport

I spotted a U.S. Postal Service drop box and began to weep. I know that must seem silly to you but it symbolized home to me and I was overcome with emotion."

"In the ensuing years we have passed through customs scores of times upon our return to the United States, still each time we do, Melba eagerly waits for the immigration official to stamp her passport and then look up and say, 'Welcome home.'"

Struggling to control his emotions, he said. "When Daddy took his last breath I knew I had lost an irretrievable part of myself. The man who gave me life was gone and it felt like I had a hole in my heart. On another level I rejoiced for I knew Daddy was more alive than he had ever been and even as I wept with grief I rejoiced for him. With the eye of faith I saw Daddy getting his passport stamped at Heaven's gate. I could almost hear Jesus say, 'Welcome home, Dick Exley, welcome home!'"

It gives me great joy to recall Don's words, and more especially to know that Dad is no longer a "resident alien" in this world of pain, but *a full fledged citizen of Heaven and a member of that great cloud of witnesses.* [37] Of course this does not eliminate the pain of our loss but it does put it into perspective. Even as we grieve, we are comforted with the knowledge that one day we will be reunited never to part.

Good-bye Daddy. In life you taught me how to live and in death you have shown me how to die with dignity. I will always be in your debt. Your finger prints are all over my life.

Appendix

PRAYERS FOR THOSE WHO GRIEVE

A Prayer to Pray When the Prognosis is Grim

Lord Jesus, help us, for our world has been turned upside down. The test results are not good. The doctor's prognosis is grim and fierce winds of doubt and fear roar, threatening our faith. Remind us, Lord, that while he/she is our loved one, they are also Your son/daughter. That while we love him/her deeply, You love him/her more. Teach us to trust Your love and to say with people of all ages, *"The Lord doeth all things well. Blessed be the name of the Lord."* Amen.

A Prayer to Pray When You Can't Feel God's Presence

Lord Jesus, the funeral is over, the last of the family and friends have departed, and I have never felt more alone. You promised to be with us, to never leave us, or forsake us but I can't sense your presence. I try to pray but the words get stuck in my throat. Help me Lord, for I cannot help myself. Intercede for me, for grief has made me mute. May Your strength be made perfect in my weakness. In Your holy name I pray. Amen.

A Prayer to Pray When Grief Tempts You to be Angry

Lord Jesus, I don't want to feel this way but I can't seem to help myself. I lie awake in the dark and relive everything that has happened and I seethe with anger. I want to blame someone. I want to punish someone but there's no one to hold responsible. Only You hold the power of life and death and I dare not accuse You, yet in my heart of hearts it's You I hold responsible. With one hand I shove You away and with the other I cling to You for dear life. Help me to trust You even if I cannot understand Your ways for You are my only hope, my only help. In Your holy name I pray. Amen.

A Prayer for Assurance

Lord Jesus, hear my prayer for I'm blind with grief. Never have I felt so alone. My pain is unrelenting, the future hopeless, a black hole. After months of grieving I'm tempted to think it will never end. And I'm tired, so terribly tired. Only You can help me. It's not answers I need but assurance. Assure me of Your nearness. Let me sense Your presence, be nearer to me than the breath I breathe, more real than life itself. Assure me of Your unfailing love and Your purpose for my life. Don't let this terrible pain be wasted. Redeem it somehow and use it to help others and further Your Kingdom. Fulfill Your purpose in my life and restore my joy. Do this by the mighty power of Your Holy Spirit. In Your holy name I pray. Amen.

A Prayer for Gratefulness

Lord Jesus, redeem my memories. Deliver me from thoughts of sickness and death. Replace these painful recollections with the joyous memories of the life we shared. Turn my grief into gratefulness that I may praise You all the days of my life for You are my Lord and my God and You are worthy of all praise. In Your holy name I pray. Amen.

A Prayer of Thanksgiving

Lord Jesus, I want to thank You for all the good memories I have. I thank You for rare and tender moments—falling in love and getting married, giving birth, becoming a grandparent, growing old with the one I love. I thank You for a good marriage where love was true. I thank You for the gift of family, for three generation holidays and the running laughter of healthy grandchildren. I thank You for the comfort of friends and the strength of Scripture in the dark hour of unspeakable need. I thank You for Your faithfulness and the promise of Your presence. I thank You for turning my grief into gratefulness and I will praise You all the days of my life. In Your holy name I pray. Amen.

ENDNOTES

1 Acts 10:34.

2 2 Corinthians 1:3, 4.

3 2 Corinthians 7:6.

4 See Psalm 46:1.

5 Luke 9:60.

6 Reb Dovid Din: *An oral tradition cited in Hasidic Tales,* quoted in *Prayer: Does It Make Any Difference?* by Philip Yancey (Grand Rapids: Zondervan, 2006), p.68.

7 John 11:3.

8 John 11:17.

9 John 11:21.

10 John 11:27.

11 John 11:24.

12 John 11:25, 26.

13 John 11:32, 33,35.

14 Hebrews 4:15.

15 Hebrews 4:15.

16 Psalm 51:17.

17 Romans 5:12.

18 1 John 2:12.

[19] 2 Corinthians 5:17.

[20] Luke 24:30-32.

[21] Luke 24:32.

[22] Psalm 23:4 (author emphasis).

[23] John 14:16.

[24] 1 Corinthians 15:54.

[25] Sue Monk Kidd, quoted in *Dawnings, Finding God's Light in the Darkness,* edited by Phyllis Hobe (New York: Guideposts Associates, Inc., 1981), p. 88.

[26] 2 Corinthians 5:6-8.

[27] Matthew 22:30.

[28] Matthew 17:1-6.

[29] Luke 16:19-26.

[30] Sheldon Vanauken, *A Severe Mercy* (New York: Harper & Row Publishers, 1977), p. 205.

[31] Matthew 26:26-29.

[32] John Claypool, *Tracks of a Fellow Struggler* (Nashville: Word Publishing, 1974), p. 82-83.

[33] Hebrews 13:15.

[34] Psalm 30:11.

[35] Psalm 30:5.

[36] John 14:3.

[37] Heb. 12:1.

ABOUT THE AUTHOR

Richard Exley, is the author of thirty books, many of them bestsellers, most recently *Man of Valor* and *The Alabaster Cross. The Making of a Man* was a finalist for the prestigious Gold Medallion Award.

His rich and diversified background has included serving as senior pastor of churches in Colorado and Oklahoma, as well as hosting several popular radio programs, including the nationally syndicated *Straight from the Heart.*

When not traveling the country as a speaker, Richard and his wife, Brenda Starr, spend their time in a secluded cabin overlooking picturesque Beaver Lake in Northwest Arkansas.

Richard enjoys quiet talks with old friends, kerosene lamps, good books, a warm fire when it is cold, and a good cup of coffee any time. He's an avid Denver Broncos fan, an aspiring bass fisherman, and an amateur photographer.

To write the author or to schedule speaking engagements, seminars, as well as, men's and couple's retreats, you can contact the author by visiting his website at: www.richardexleyministries.org

You are also invited to listen to the author's daily *Straight From the Heart* podcast, also available on his website.

Additional copies of this book and
other titles by Richard Exley can be ordered
from your local bookstore.

The Alabaster Cross

Man of Valor

Encounters with Christ

Encounters at the Cross (coming soon!)

If this book has touched your life,
we would love to hear from you.

Please write us at:

Vallew Press

P.O. Box 35327

Tulsa, Oklahoma 74153-0327

VALLEW
PRESS